A PERSONAL PRAYER BOOK

PERSONAL PRAYERS

Brief prayers for morning and
evening designed to help people
learn how to speak to God
in a simple way.

ALLAN W. SCHREIBER

DIMENSIONS
FOR LIVING
NASHVILLE

MORNING

Thank you, God—
   for a new day, a day in which I can enjoy the life
      you have given me;
   for the comfort you give me: that during all this
      day I am your very own, because Jesus has
      restored me to you and forgiven all my sins.

Help me—
   to live this day in the best way and with a right
      spirit;
   to approach my work cheerfully and to do my
      tasks faithfully;
   to be courteous and kind to the people I meet;
   to be more patient in times of disappointment,
      when I am frustrated and things don't seem to
      go right;
   to keep control of myself and not lose my temper;
   to accept praise with modesty, and criticism with-
      out anger;
   to remain calm throughout the day.

I ask this for Jesus' sake. Amen.

EVENING   Day 1

Thank you, God, for nighttime and for time to rest.

I made many mistakes today, Lord; please forgive me
and cleanse me before I go to rest. I'm sorry that
I so often lose patience both with myself and
with others. Heal anyone that I may have hurt
today. I'm sorry, Lord.

Now bless all those I love; keep them from all harm
and danger;

Bless my friends, and the people with whom I work;
let nothing come between us to spoil our friendship.

Bless all those who are ill; give them restful sleep
tonight, and give them your healing love.

Bless all the sad and lonely people, and comfort
them.

Bless me, my family, and all my loved ones, this
night. Thank you so much for Jesus; now we
can sleep in peace, assured of your great love for
us now and always.

All this I ask in Jesus' name. Amen.

Good morning, Lord!

Thank you for rest and refreshment, and the new
day, and all your wonderful gifts to us.

As I become aware of things I do that annoy my family or friends, help me to avoid them. As I
become aware of things that please my family
and friends, help me to remember to do them.

Lord, you know how often I open my big mouth
and speak before I think; help me today to overcome that weakness, so that I don't hurt or
embarrass anyone.

If I feel compelled today to disagree with someone
else, please help me to do so in kindness and
courtesy.

If anyone today has good reason to find fault with
me, help me to accept the correction as if it
came from you, my dear heavenly Lord.

Help me during this day—
    to consider the feelings of others as much as I
    think of my own;
    to keep growing more aware of the presence of
    Jesus with me, so that I may live more as he
    would want me to live.

I pray in his name. Amen.

Another day is over, Lord—a day of work in which I have enjoyed your company. Thank you, Lord, for a good day!

In quietness now I come to you, to speak with you and to feel your presence. As I think of your wonderful love to me, I am greatly humbled; I am aware of so many things in my life just today that should bring your anger upon me rather than your love.

Lord, bless all the wonderful people who are thinking of me and praying for me tonight:
my family, my friends, my loved ones;
those who have no one to remember them, no one to pray for them;
those in illness or pain, the dying, the bereaved, the bewildered;
those bound up in the chains of drugs or alcohol;
those who have been driven to despair.

Lord, where our sin has made a rotten mess of so many wonderful people, have mercy on us!

Bless me as I go to rest. Give me sorrow for my sins, a grateful heart for all your gifts, and the joy of knowing all is at peace with you because Jesus has given me your peace.

Hear this prayer for Jesus' sake. Amen.

MORNING

Lord, sometimes when I wake up, I wonder what happened to the night because it seemed to pass so quickly. But I still thank you for a new day of life and opportunity.

Today, I am going to try very hard to keep all negative ideas out of my mind, and to think your thoughts and try to do your will. Help me to do this.

Help me today—
- to see quickly all the opportunities where I can praise others;
- to be patient with those I would so easily condemn;
- to be aware of all the opportunities where I can extend the same loving forgiveness as you have given to me;
- to stop and count to ten before I hand out harsh criticism.

Give me control today so that the old nature in me will stay drowned, and the new nature rise to do what is right. Then I will have control over my temper, be slow to anger, speak no hasty words, and be a more lovable person.

So help me today, Lord, that I may help everyone and hurt no one.

For Jesus' sake. Amen.

*O*God, thank you for the assurance that I am your very own, purchased and won back from sin, death, and the devil through the life, death, and resurrection of Jesus, your Son, my Lord.

I come to you as a little child, telling you that I enjoyed today; but I didn't do all those things I said I wanted to do. Please forgive me! I know you understand, you love, and you forgive.

As I lie down to sleep, relax the tensions of my body and my mind. Calm me down, and remove the thoughts that worry and perplex me.

Help me to unload all my cares on you, because you have told me I'm much more important than the sparrows, which never fall without your knowledge.

As I go to sleep, I ask that you will renew the strength of my body for my work tomorrow, refresh my mind so that I will think thoughts that are good, and remove any worries and give me your peace.

I look to you, O God, for all strength, for in you I trust.

This I ask through my Lord Jesus Christ. Amen.

Ogod, you are my God; early in the morning I come to you. My soul is thirsting for you; my whole being desires you.

O God, it is so easy for me to neglect this time of prayer each day. Sometimes I sleep late, and I am tempted to believe there is no time left to talk with you. Help me to keep my priorities right.

As I go out into the busy world today, I need your power and your direction.

Give to me—
humility so that I do not exaggerate my own importance;
graciousness and gentleness so that I am a better person to live with;
consistency of effort and reliability so that I do my work well;
alertness so that I can see quickly how to help those around me;
your love so that I can understand how others feel, and be able to help them;
the continual awareness of your presence so that I may consciously try to do your will.

For Jesus' sake. Amen.

Evening   Day 4

Thank you, God, for a good day and for all the help you have given me.

Not everything went as well as it should have; but, considering who I am, I am not greatly surprised. It is good for me, Lord, to consider who I am and what I am. With sorrow I realize I am a miserable sinner; but with great joy I realize I am your dear saint, covered by Jesus your Son, who took my place in his life for me and in his bitter death for me.

As I think on these things I want to thank you, God—
for watching over me all through today;
for helping me in all my work today;
for giving me strength to overcome any temptations through today;
for all the kindness I received today;
for my home, family, and friends who loved me today;
for all the help and sympathy that was shown me today.

Help me now to lie down to sleep tonight, tired, but with a glad and grateful heart.

I ask this in Jesus' name. Amen.

OGod, as I begin this new day, I thank you that you are our shelter and strength, always ready to help in times of trouble. No matter what comes upon me in the course of this day, I will not be afraid.

Help me to dedicate my life to you this day, and to
remember that, since I am your precious child, I
can claim your power and promises at every
moment.

Help me—
to live to you this day, doing those things that are
good and honest;
to avoid those things that could lead me into the
pathway of sin;
to be a comfort to those who are sad, a friend to
the lonely, an encouragement to the down-
hearted, and a help to all who are in difficulty;
to live this day so that I do not cause others to
worry, let down others who trust me, or hurt
those who are close to me.

So grant that others may see in me at least a small
reflection of my master Jesus, whose I am, and
whom I love to serve.

In his name I pray. Amen.

Evening   Day 5

To be at home in the evening is good, dear Lord.

As I think of that joy of home, I also think of the joy
    when I go to the house of the Lord to worship
    you, my God.

Forgive me for anytime I have neglected your pre-
    cious Word and the worship of your house on
    Sunday. It is just so easy for us to get so busy
    with the things of life that we forget about life
    itself.

Thank you, God, that you understand us so well,
    and that your thoughts to us are full of love and
    peace.

Forgive me—
    if today I made trouble for anyone, especially
    among my own loved ones;
    if I made work harder for anyone by being unkind
    or unreasonable, slack or inefficient;
    if I was self-willed and stubborn, and so caused
    trouble for my friends and dear ones.

Help me tomorrow to be more aware of my failures,
    more loving and understanding toward others,
    so that I might be more of the kind of person
    you want me to be.

For Jesus' sake I pray. Amen.

O God, it is wonderful to wake up in the morning and to realize that I am a very special person.

I may not look or feel very special so early in the morning, but I know that you sent Jesus from the heavenly throne to live and die for me and all people, and that is why I know I am special to you.

God, I am going to be very busy today, just as on all other days, but help me to remember during today who I am.

Help me—
    to see your beauty in the world around me, so that I stop and say, "Thank you,"
    to hear your voice when you speak to me;
    to hear the cries of those who are calling for my help;
    to pause sometimes during the day just to think and remember;
    to see the needs of my family, friends, and dear ones, and to meet those needs with love.

O God, I want to do my best today.

This I ask in Jesus' precious name. Amen.

Thank you, Lord, for preserving us this day from all dangers.

The darkness has fallen over the earth, but preserve us from all the darkness of sin that our old enemy would try to bring upon us. As we take off our clothes, may we also remove all earthly cares and worries, so that we may sleep in peace.

Lord, there were many things today that were not the best in every way, so I ask your forgiveness. Hide all my failures as in the darkness of this night, so that they are gone from your sight.

I know they are gone forever because Jesus has removed the sins of all by his death; through him I can rest in peace with you.

Having freed me of any more worry about my sins, free me, as I lie down, from worry about my work, money, temptation, health, family, and other earthly things.

Help me to remember that worrying only makes things worse, and that worry is a denial of my trust in you.

Give me your peace in my troubled heart tonight, through Jesus Christ my Lord. Amen.

Every morning, Lord, your mercies are new.

Thank you for today. My mind is thinking of Jesus
who died for me on the terrible cross, so that I
might find peace and rest for my soul.

I praise and thank you, Lord, that you have given
me the glorious gift of salvation.

Cover me, dear Lord Jesus, with your grace, and
remove from me all the stain of my sin.

Jesus, help me to walk with you all through this day.

Give to me—
some of the great wisdom that is in your words;
some of the love that is in your heart;
some of the help that is in your hands.

Fill me with your great patience with people, and
with your great love that is able to forgive and
love even those who are against us.

Help me to live this day as your follower, living in
your company, so that others may see—even
though rather dimly—your presence in me.

I ask this for Jesus' sake. Amen.

EVENING

To come to the end of the day resting in your peace, O God, is so wonderful. As I lay aside my working clothes and my work, I realize how you have blessed me during today.

I also wish to lay aside the sins of this day: where I have been lazy, where I have been proud in my own opinions, where I have hurt someone with words that were not kind or thoughtful, where I have had thoughts that would bring me shame if other people saw them. I also confess that there are many other things which I really ought to have done but didn't get around to doing.

Please forgive me and make me clean.

Dear Lord, life runs away so quickly. Help me—
to number my days, that I may get a heart of wisdom;
to make good use of the many opportunities that you lay before me for helping others and serving you.

As I go to sleep tonight, help me—
to remember that I am one of your precious saints;
to think good thoughts and relax in your presence, assured of your protection.

Bless all my loved ones, too, as we rest this night.

In Jesus' name I pray. Amen.

MORNING

Good morning, Lord!

Thank you for rest and refreshment! You are the
    Lord of all life!

Lead me during this day to get to know you a little
    better.

Help me—
    to do my work more carefully and diligently;
    to help other people more lovingly;
    to grow to be more like Jesus.

Give me the strength, dear Lord, to make some more
    progress in my life, to become more like the per-
    son you want me to be.

Dear Lord, sometimes I forget the wonderful things
    you have done for me, as well as the wonderful
    things you have planned for me in the future.

Help me to remember these things better today.

For Jesus' sake. Amen.

EVENING

O Lord, the day is over, and I come to you to have this little talk before I go to rest.

Forgive me, Lord—
   for not always doing the things I had planned to do, the good things I forgot to do;
   for not giving the loving help at work or at home that I ought to give;
   for being so wrapped up in my own little world that I didn't see the opportunities for loving others the way you wanted me to;
   for being so selfish with my own leisure time and my own comforts that I could not give them up to help others, or to help your church, your people, or your work.

Help me—
   to learn that selfishness and happiness cannot exist together;
   to discover your joy by losing myself and bringing love, help, and happiness to others.

Through Jesus Christ my Lord. Amen.

MORNING

O Lord, you are my light and my salvation; I will fear no one.

I have asked the Lord for one thing; one thing only do I want: to live in the Lord's house all my life, to marvel at his goodness, and to ask his guidance there.

Because of Jesus and his life, death, and resurrection, I will never fear. I will trust you, dear God, now and always.

The devil and other people will try to draw me away from you, but I call on you to help me and deliver me.

I know you will keep me safe all through this day, dear God.

I will sing. I will praise the Lord.

Bless me and all my loved ones as we begin this day; and as we begin, so may we end it together— with you, dear Lord.

I pray in Jesus' name. Amen.

EVENING

Thank you, Lord, for the many blessings of this day of my life.

I realize that I am now one day nearer to coming
     home to be with you forever.

At the end of this day, give me peace of mind so
     that I can rest in true peace.

Take away all the sins that troubled me this day: all
     envy, resentment, bitterness, anger, foolish
     worry, and all those things that were not as
     good as they should have been.

Help me now to lie down in real peace:
     at peace with myself—knowing that Jesus covers
     me, and I am your child;
     at peace with others—holding no bitterness
     against anyone, and forgiving others as you
     have forgiven me;
     at peace with you—knowing your constant love is
     with me, as I put my hope and trust in you.

In Jesus' name I pray. Amen.

MORNING

Thank you, O God, for the rest of this past night and the gift of this new day.

Give me wisdom and understanding, so that I can live this day as I ought. If temptations come my way, help me to overcome each one in the strength that Jesus gives me.

Give to me—
the strength to do each task that is given to me, so that I can do it well;
the strength to face the responsibilities of life that confront me this day;
the wisdom to speak when words are needed, and to be silent when silence is required;
the wisdom to know when I ought to speak my mind, and when I ought to hold my peace.

Help me to come to the end of this day with the joy that I have lived the day with you, my God. Amen.

Dear Lord Jesus, it is so wonderful to have you as my friend, my Savior, and my Lord.

Thank you for the Holy Spirit, by whose power I
    have come to realize your great love for me.

Thank you—
    for all the friends who have enriched my life;
    for all the people with whom I have had fellow-
      ship today in so many different ways;
    for the enjoyment of music, radio, and television,
      and the opportunity for recreation and fresh air;
    for the warmth of love, for those who are most
      near and dear to me;
    for those whose loving hands serve my needs and
      care for my comfort.

Give me peace and rest as I close my eyes this night.

For Jesus' sake. Amen.

MORNING

Dear Lord, I wake up and realize how quickly time is flying.

Teach me to number my days carefully, so that I can be wise in how best to use them. This is another day of opportunity; so I ask you now to help me see the opportunities you send and to use them wisely.

Help me, Lord, not to get too wrapped up in thinking about myself, but to think first of others.

Bless those for whom today is not going to be an easy day:
   those who are facing big decisions;
   those who are struggling with temptation;
   those who have great problems to solve;
   those who need your special power to help them this day.

Bless those for whom today is going to be a very sad day:
   those who have lost a loved one;
   those who have lost their marriage partner;
   those who have lost their children;
   those who are unemployed, still looking for work.

Bless those for whom today is going to be a happy day. May their happiness spill over on to others, so that together we may enjoy that happiness that comes from you.

Help me, O Lord, to bear the burdens of others, even as Jesus has carried all my burdens, and relieved me with his love. Amen.

Thank you, God, for today.

Thank you—
   for the health, strength, and ability to work that
      you gave me;
   for those who are my friends, those who care for
      me, love me, and pray for me;
   for those times when you enabled me to over-
      come any temptation; when you made it possi-
      ble for me to choose the right and refuse the
      wrong; when you spoke to me and made me
      very much aware of your presence and your
      guidance.

I thank you for Jesus:
   for his great love for me;
   for the forgiveness of sins through his death and
      resurrection;
   for his presence with me;
   for the friendship I have with you because of him.

Help me to show my gratitude by love and obedi-
      ence to you and by service to others.

In Jesus' name. Amen.

As I wake up this day, Lord, I remember how quickly time passes by.

I give you thanks that my life has not been wasted, because I now know your plan for life as it is to be lived in your company.

Forgive me, Lord, if I sometimes live as though I were not aware of your wonderful presence.

Help me to do today all that I need to do; trouble me if I try to put off until tomorrow what I really ought to do today.

Strengthen me to face the tasks of this day in the right spirit.

Give me patience when things go wrong, and especially understanding with other people.

Forgive me, dear Lord, when I behave as if I am the only one who is right and everyone else is wrong. Help me to grow to be more like you, my blessed Lord.

I pray in your name. Amen.

EVENING   Day 12

Dear Jesus, you remember better than I do the good resolutions I had as I went out into the world this morning. Now at evening, as I look back, I wish I had remembered them more during the day.

Please forgive my failures and bless my poor efforts.

As this day ends, I want to thank you again, my
  Savior and Lord, for your continual forgiveness,
  even though I keep falling into the same holes
  so often.

Thank you for giving me and all your people the
  assurance that your patience, kindness, mercy,
  and love never end.

Help me now to go to rest with calmness and peace.

Bless all my dear ones. May we all rest in peace and
  find joy in your company every day.

This I ask for your love's sake. Amen.

Dear God, another day has dawned, a day of opportunity to show my love for you by reflecting your love in all I do.

Help me to love those who are nearest and dearest to me. So often I discover that, because I know them so well, I say and do things to them which I would never say or do to others.

Thank you for all the wonderful gifts you have given me, especially my home, my family, my friends, my work, my church family, my country.

Help me to remember in prayer those for whom life is not nearly so happy as it is for me:
all refugees who have no home or place to call their own;
all Christians in lands where Christians are persecuted;
all who are unhappy in their work, who are badly paid, or have to work in poor conditions;
all who are badly treated in their home and family;
all who are without friends—the lonely, the sick, the sad, those in hospitals.

O God, help me never to become blind and heartless to the needs of others around me.

For Jesus' sake I ask this. Amen.

How wonderful it is, dear Lord, to stop at the end of a day's work and relax in your company!

I do appreciate your love for me; help me always to respond to your love in a way that is genuine, that is according to your will.

Thank you for the wonderful certainty that Jesus has taken my sins away and has opened the door to heaven for me.

Forgive me—
when I was too impatient today, especially with people;
when I became a nuisance for others especially by trying to prove that I was right and they were wrong;
when I hurt someone's feelings even if I didn't realize it at the time;
when I judged too quickly and lacked in mercy and patience.

Remove these and all other dark spots of sin, and help me to grow more loving and kind, more like Jesus.

In his name I pray. Amen.

Morning

Dear Lord in heaven, as I am about to go out on life's way this new day, help me to appreciate this world's beauty, the warmth of the sun, the color of the trees and flowers, the fresh air, the glimpses of all lovely things.

Thank you for helping me to know the great value you have placed on me.

I know you have great plans for me, and I know how hard the devil tries to make me despair of my poor efforts so that I might give up.

Thank you for never giving up on me. For this I'll praise you forever.

As I go out to work, help me—
to remember the sin and evil of this world;
to keep looking ahead to see the danger areas and to avoid them;
to overcome temptations, and so make my life a witness to others.

If anyone near me falls into trouble, let me love rather than judge and condemn.

Be with me, Lord, so that when evening comes, I may know that this day has been a well-spent gift of your grace.

Through Jesus Christ my Lord. Amen.

Dear God, tonight I come to you with all I am and all I have.

I come to you with:
 all my sins, seeking your forgiveness;
 all my hopes, aims, and ambitions, seeking your
   blessing;
 all my tasks, duties, and responsibilities, seeking
   your help;
 all my friends and loved ones, seeking your love,
   care, and protection.

And I come with a thankful and believing heart,
   confessing my appreciation for all you have
   done for me.

Thank you, dear Jesus, for sharing this time with me
   in such a special way this evening.

Let me rest in peace, knowing that you are my
   shelter now and always. Amen.

MORNING

Dear Lord Jesus, I praise you for your rich blessings to me and my loved ones.

We have so much to be thankful for, and it is so easy to overlook those blessings or to take them for granted.

My old human nature is still active. I would love it to be eliminated from my life forever, but I realize that will happen only in the life to come.

And so I need your help again:
to live my faith joyfully in all I do and say;
to show gratitude to those to whom I owe so much;
to do my work with proper responsibility and reliability;
to gain the mastery when temptation comes to defeat me;
to be alert to the needs of those near me;
to give a good witness by doing God's will this day;
to show kindness, consideration, and acceptance even to those who are difficult to live with.

So may I be transformed by the power of your Spirit to be the person you want me to be.

For your love's sake. Amen.

D ear Lord in heaven, I thank you for the guidance of your Holy Spirit, who comes to me through your blessed Word and Holy Communion.

Through his power in these means, I enjoy the real
     presence of Jesus in my life, and I am constantly
     being renewed in his love, forgiveness, patience,
     understanding, endurance, and other great gifts.

Forgive me whenever I have neglected this wonder-
     ful source of power, thus depriving myself of the
     growth the Spirit wants to give me.

Thank you for being so patient with me, so that I
     am not lost or ever driven from your presence.

Keep me in such reverence and awe that I will never
     wander from you.

Thank you for today, for all the happiness I enjoyed,
     for all the love and friendship.

Forgive me for all that was wrong in what I did
     today, all that grieved others and hurt you.

Give me now a quiet and restful night.

For Jesus' sake. Amen.

Dear Lord God, to know you is so wonderful. This is life eternal that begins now and will continue with you forever.

Let me know you better each day, that I may enjoy life in all its fullness, and may see more clearly your will and plan for my life.

Help me to meet you often in your Word, and to encounter the presence of Jesus in the Holy Communion.

Give me a greater awareness of my sin, and a greater appreciation of your love and forgiveness.

Dear God, make me realize that true freedom lies in following Jesus and walking in his steps. Then I will know the joy of not being under the bondage of sin, but under your gracious and loving control. Give me strength to live this day that I may come closer to loving you as you have loved me.

In Jesus' name I pray. Amen.

Dear Lord, this morning I wanted your help to make me a little more loving.

Thank you for your help; please forgive my failures.

Forgive me—
   for thinking thoughts that were not good for me;
   for speaking words that I should never have
      allowed to pass my lips;
   for walking too close to temptation so that the
      devil had a chance to attack me;
   for all the wrong things which I know I have
      done, the wrong things I am not even aware of,
      and the many failures to do good things I ought
      to have done.

Give me, before I go to rest, the assurance of being
      forgiven, knowing the peace that only Jesus can
      give.

This I ask for Jesus' sake. Amen.

As I begin this day of opportunity, I want to thank you, Lord, for being so kind, gracious, understanding, and forgiving toward me.

I realize that in no way do I deserve your great love and generosity. Help me to make this day a continual offering of thanks and praise for all you do for me.

Show that same love and kindness to other people for whom today is going to have difficulties:
  those in hospitals, especially those facing major surgery;
  those who have important decisions to make for the future;
  those who face tests or examinations;
  those who are unemployed, or who begin new work today;
  those who are facing big issues in their lives that need your guidance and blessing.

Bless all your people; and bless me as I go out to this day's work, so that in your strength I may do your will and come to the end of this day without regrets; through Jesus Christ my Lord. Amen.

Dear God, I thank you that through Jesus I have met you and experienced your great mercy and love.

Thank you—
  for every new thing I discovered today, everything
    that added to my store of knowledge;
  for the people I met during this day, and the fel-
    lowship I have enjoyed with them, especially
    those who are your special people;
  for all relatives and for the friends in our church
    family, with whom we enjoy life together in
    your company;
  for the times when I was able to grow in love and
    understanding, especially with people whom I
    had not really loved or known.

People change, and the events of life keep changing;
    I thank you for Jesus who never changes, but
    who is the same yesterday, today, and forever.

Hear this my evening prayer, and fill me with your
    Holy Spirit so that I may grow to be more like
    the person you want me to be.

In Jesus' name I pray. Amen.

Dear Lord, you have refreshed me with sleep, and now I awake to follow your directions for another day.

Today I will receive many requests for help; let me never find any of these a nuisance or a burden.

As people come asking for some of my time, let me be kind and patient, cooperating with a willing spirit.

Bless those who are in my own family and the family of my local church.

May we grow in fellowship with you and each other, so that the warmth of love, and the depth of care and concern, may grow toward each other.

Help me never to be so immersed in my own work, or so fond of my own pleasures, that I am too busy or too tired to help those who need my help.

Help me to understand ever more clearly, as I am drawn closer to Jesus, that it is in losing myself that I will gain the life that is best.

This I ask for Jesus' sake. Amen.

Dear God, the thing that hurts and troubles me most as I look back on my day is the way I have not reflected your love to others today as well as I should have.

Forgive me, Lord—
  for criticizing others and being unkind;
  for laughing at people;
  for thinking other people fools, and for putting myself above them;
  for any request that I refused when I should not have;
  for any sympathy I did not give;
  for anything I did that may have hurt another's feelings.

Lord God, you are so patient and forgiving toward me; help me to be the same toward others. I know I will grow that way if I let Jesus come to me every day.

Spirit of God, let me now be assured of forgiveness and eternal life with God, so that I may rest in peace and rise to give glory to you tomorrow.

In Jesus' name I pray. Amen.

God, because we are your dear children, I come before you with confidence at the beginning of this day to say: "Good morning!"

I don't know what this day will bring me, even
    though my plans are made; and so I ask that,
    whatever does happen today, I will sense your
    presence, and be strengthened to do whatever I
    am called to do.

Give me the faith, dear God, to know that you are
    working in all things for good to those who love
    you, even if those things don't appear good to
    me at first sight.

Give me patience this day—
    with my work, so that I'll work at it until it is
    done well, no matter how difficult or boring it
    may seem;
    with people, so that I will not get annoyed or lose
    my temper;
    with my life, so that I do not give up hope, but
    catch a glimpse of the great potential you see in
    me as your new creation.

Hear this my morning prayer for Jesus' sake. Amen.

God of mercy, as I come to the end of this day, I know (and you know better than I) that many of my good intentions and plans were not fulfilled. Forgive me for my weakness, and cleanse me from all my faults.

Thank you for your love and forgiveness so that I can go to rest in peace, knowing the great comfort that, whether I live or die, I am yours.

There are many people for whom this night will be terribly long and dreary; I ask you to give them rest and peace.

There are many who will spend these hours in great loneliness; I ask you to comfort them with your presence and to keep their hopes alive.

There are many who this night are sad because they have lost someone they loved very dearly; help them to have someone to share their sadness and to bring them consolation.

There are many who will go to sleep not knowing you at all, not aware of their eternal danger; I ask that you will open their lives so that I or another Christian may speak to them and show them your love in Jesus our Savior.

All this I ask in his name. Amen.

Lord, it is good to be alive in your world today.

I know it is easy for me to find sin, troubles, problems, cruelty, bitterness, and many other terrible things; but I know there are also wonderful things happening around me and even within me, which give me reason to thank and praise you, my God.

Thank you for helping me to grow by the power of your Spirit as I meditate on your Word at home and in my church, and as I receive Jesus in bread and wine at Holy Communion.

I know that because of my old sinful nature I do not grow as I should. But I praise you that this old nature was first drowned in my baptism, and I pray that each day it may be put to death so that the wonderful new creation in me can grow and be formed into the very likeness of Jesus himself.

Lord, I pray that all your people will grow more conscious of your great love and experience its power, so that we all become the kind of people you want us to be.

Help me this day to be a help and example to others and to bring strength and encouragement, wherever I may be; through Jesus Christ my Lord. Amen.

*O*God, at the end of the day, it is not the things I have done which worry me but rather the things I did not get done. Please accept my repentance and forgive me.

Forgive me for my failures today:
> where I did not do my best, or my work was shoddy, or I didn't help others as much as I could;
> where I did not speak the words of praise, encouragement, and thanks that I should have;
> where I failed to express love and to extend courtesy and graciousness to those with whom I live and work.

Thank you for Jesus, his life for me, his death for me, whereby I can have complete assurance of your forgiveness and complete confidence that all is well between us.

Help me each day to do better, to grow in knowing and doing your will, so that each night I may have fewer regrets.

Let me now rest in peace.

In Jesus' name I pray all this. Amen.

Thank you, God, for a brand new day.

As I wake, I realize that I am one day closer to the end of my time on this earth, but also one day closer to seeing you, my God and Lord.

Help me to use today—and every day—as you want me to use it.

Make me aware of whatever gifts and strengths you have given me, and help me to use them in honoring you and in serving others, wherever I am.

Make me aware that all the money and other earthly gifts that pass through my hands are yours for me and mine to use. Let me grow in the generosity that comes from you.

Help me—
    to use my time wisely in honest work;
    to be ready to use some of my spare time for others, too, and not only for my own pleasure;
    to grow as the new creation that I already am in Christ.

In his name I pray. Amen.

Thank you, Lord, for the daytime and the night-time to work and to rest.

Before I go to rest, I think of Jesus and all he has done for me. Without him I would be lost; but with him I am a saint, covered by his grace, freed from the terrible guilt and curse of sin and its punishment.

Lord, bring me closer to Jesus each day.

Forgive me, Lord
for the times I did not do my best work;
for allowing myself thoughts and feelings that I should not have;
for the hasty words spoken to those around me;
for my lack of consideration to those who love me most of all;
for expecting more of my friends than I am pre-pared to give to them;
for not giving my church family my full support at all times because I am too selfish;
for running away from responsibilities and shirk-ing my duty.

Thank you for your forgiveness that I now enjoy. Because of it, I now lie down in peace and safety, in Jesus' saving name. Amen.

MORNING

Dear God in heaven, I come into your presence to be quiet and still and to know that you are God.

I pray that from this time of prayer I may take with me your quiet serenity and peace, to be with me through the rough-and-tumble of this day's life.

I come—
asking for your wisdom, so that today I may not make foolish mistakes;
asking for your peace to fill me, so that I will not become worried or upset during this day;
asking for your love, which is mine in Jesus, to work in me so that throughout this day nothing may make me bitter or unforgiving or unkind.

Dear God, let me begin this new day with you, continue it with you, and end it with you, so that I shall know at its end that I have walked with you.

Hear this my morning prayer for Jesus' sake. Amen.

Dear God, the perfect world you created has ended up in a tangled mess, and all around us we see how the old enemy is causing terrible trouble. Part of that tangled mess is in my life, too. My old nature drags me down so often. I fail to let the new rise within me. For this I ask your forgiveness.

O God, as I get into difficulties and make mistakes again and again, it would be so easy to blame others; those with whom I work, those in my own home, or those in my church family, and to say that it was not all my fault. But I don't want to say that, because it would not really be true. All I need to say, and all I want to say, is: Forgive me, Lord; help me not to be discouraged, not to give up the battle of striving for what is right, and help me to do better tomorrow.

As I go to rest, give me peace of mind, calmness in my body, and let me find that rest which refreshes and restores me for my work tomorrow.

This I ask for Jesus' sake. Amen.

Morning

Thank you, Lord, for waking me to face a new day. Surround me with your presence, and equip me for its tasks and challenges.

Some days I wake up feeling wonderful; on other days I wake up feeling really miserable and like running away. There are jobs I don't want to do; there are people I don't want to meet. I don't always feel ready or able to cope with all I have to do. But you know, as I know, that I can't run and hide. Life has to go on, no matter how I feel about it.

Lord Jesus, by your cross and resurrection, you freed me from all my sin and trouble. And you know all about me and my life on this earth, because you lived here as one of us. Come and be with me today, and help me to feel you beside me all the time, so that I will not merely last out grimly to the end of this day, but may know the joy of living with you.

You came to give us life in great abundance; help me to experience that more fully during this day.

In your saving name I pray. Amen.

Dear Lord, tonight I come to you to ask you to
bless me, my friends, and all my loved ones.

Bless all those whose lives are woven together with
   mine, those who are so important to me that
   my life would never be the same without them.

Bless all who have helped me to grow in my love for
   you, those without whom my life would be so
   much the poorer.

Dear Lord, watch over your chosen ones.

Give your gifts of love and wisdom to all parents so
   that they may bring up their children in a loving relationship with you and with each other.

Bless all children that they may grow with you in
   such a way that they will honor their parents,
   and discover the wonderful potential that you
   have prepared for them in their lives.

Thank you, Lord, for today, for all that happened—
   whether I was able to see that it was all for my
   good, or whether I failed to see how you were
   being good to me in things I thought were hard
   to bear.

For all your love and mercy, I thank and praise you
   now. Amen.

God in heaven, I praise you that I have been given the privilege of calling you Lord. Because you have given me the blessing of knowing Jesus as my Savior, I can begin this day with the complete confidence that all things will work together for my good.

Help me today—
   to be more appreciative of others;
   to remember to say thank you for everything that is
      done for me and never to take things for granted;
   to be ready to give you praise and glory all day
      long, because I know you are always guiding
      and directing things for my advantage, even
      when I cannot see how that can be. Lord, I do
      not ask to see; I simply ask that you will give
      me faith to trust you in all things.

Make me aware when people around me are lonely,
   depressed, discouraged, and unhappy. Open my
   eyes when someone is feeling left out of things.
   And show me at these times how to be a caring
   and loving person, just as Jesus would have
   been in such situations.

Lord Jesus, all through this day help me to see people with your eyes and to love them with your love; to your praise and honor. Amen.

O God, at the end of this day I ask you to forgive me for all my forgetfulness and disobedience of you, and for any trouble I may have caused others.

Forgive me—
  if I made a nuisance of myself by being stubborn,
    or unwilling to let others correct me, or being
    unnecessarily fussy;
  if I have wasted other people's time by being late
    and keeping them waiting, or by being careless
    and slow with my work;
  if I have annoyed other people, especially the
    ones I love;
  if I have been cross, irritable, bad tempered, or
    discourteous;
  if I have refused to see no other point of view than
    my own, or if I was difficult to live with today;
  if I have failed to keep my promises, especially those
    promises of faithfulness I have made to you.

I thank you for Jesus, because in him alone you
    promise me pardon and peace.

I praise you that you call me your saint because Jesus
    covers me with all his glory. May his light shine
    through me more and more each day.

For his love's sake I pray these things. Amen.

Dear God, as I begin this new day of opportunity I want to give you great thanks.

> I thank you, LORD, with all my heart; I . . . bow down and praise your name because of your constant love and faithfulness, because you have shown that your name and your commands are supreme. . . .
> When I am surrounded by troubles,
> you keep me safe. . . .
> You will do everything you have promised. . . .
> Complete the work that you have begun.
> (Psalm 138 TEV)

Help me today so that all I do will have your approval; and, when I go wrong, comfort me with your forgiveness.

Help me—
    to grow in patience so that throughout this day I may not lose my temper . . .
    to grow in perseverance so that I may keep at a task until it is successfully completed;
    to grow in peace so that others around me will be able to see a better reflection of my master, whose I am, and whom I want to serve.

In his name I pray. Amen.

Thank you, Lord, for another day that has brought me closer to the time when you and I will meet face to face.

I praise you for the confidence you give me by the power of your Holy Spirit to know that, whether I live or whether I die, I am yours forever. Extend your banner of love over me and all my loved ones as we go to rest tonight. Let your holy angels watch over us that the old enemy may have no power to disturb our rest.

Forgive me, Lord—
  if I behaved in a way that made other people feel that I was the greatest sufferer in this world;
  if I behaved as if I were the only person to be misunderstood, misjudged, and underrated, or the only one who ever got a raw deal from life.

Forgive me for magnifying my troubles and forgetting the great blessings and talents that you give me.

Help me to see things from your point of view instead of my own, so that I may think more of others and less of myself, just as Jesus did.

In Jesus' name I go to rest asking these blessings. Amen.

Dear Lord, as this new day dawns, I remember again how quickly time is passing away, and how soon my journey of life will be completed. I thank you for giving me life, and especially that I can live each day in your company, knowing the reality of your presence now, until finally I shall see you as you are.

Thank you for Jesus and all his gifts to me!

Be with me as I go out to this day's tasks.

Give to me—
> joy in my work so that I may do it with pleasure for your sake, and not just because I need the money;
> courage to do the things that are not easy to do, the things I don't want to do;
> a gracious and gentle spirit so that I can deal gently and graciously with other people, especially those whom I find difficult to like.

Help me to be happy all through today, and so to help others to be happy too.

This I ask for Jesus' sake. Amen.

I thank you, God, for today. For some people, today was exciting and happy; for others it was rather sad; and for others it was very ordinary. Whatever it was, I know it was part of your plan for me.

I thank you that I was able to do my work. Accept it as my offering to you; please forgive me if I did less than my best.

I thank you for the people I met and whose company I enjoyed, and for my family and loved ones who support me so well.

I thank you for—
every experience of love I enjoyed today;
every correction you gave to help me become a better person;
every temptation you helped me to overcome;
every new thing I was able to learn;
every help I was able to give others;
every discovery I made that will help me in the future.

I thank you especially for Jesus, for the glorious assurance that through him I have eternal salvation as a gift, and for the Holy Spirit and his wonderful working in my life.

For all the gifts I enjoyed this day I want to praise you now. Add to them the peace of your pardon and loving care, and the gift of a restful night, for Jesus' sake. Amen.

I thank you, dear Lord, that I can look forward to another day with you, another day in fellowship with other people and in service to them.

As I think of other people I know, I am concerned that many are wandering through life not realizing who you are or where they are going. They are like sheep straying without Jesus their Shepherd. And so, Lord, help them in their lostness; and use me in whatever ways you want, so that I may be led to help them too.

I remember others, too—
those who are ill and in pain;
those in hospitals, clinics, and nursing homes;
those who are disabled or paralyzed;
those whose minds and nerves have been
impaired by the strain of living;
those who are finding life difficult to bear.

You know all the people with problems, dear Lord; assure them of your care, and meet their needs with your love.

And, even if my work seems dull, worrying, or hard, badly paid or unappreciated, help me to remember how fortunate I am to have health and strength to do it. Keep me mindful of all my blessings; make me grateful to you for them, and ready to use them for you and for others this day.

This I ask for Jesus' sake. Amen.

Dear God in heaven, I am your child, received into a wonderful relationship with you at my baptism. I want to live in praise of your love and grace to me, and yet it often seems that my greatest talent lies in my ability to mess things up.

Let me see things more from your point of view.

Help me at the end of this day—
    to unwind;
    to release the tensions that have built up during
      the day;
    to relax in body and mind.

Reassure me of your pardon and peace as I confess
    my sins to you.

Lead me—
    to see the wonderful potential you have given me
      for finding joy and fulfillment in my life;
    to give praise and glory to you;
    to cast my care on you and truly to feel your ever-
      lasting arms underneath and around me.

Grant me tonight a sleep of peace, through Jesus my
    Lord and my God. Amen.

Gracious God, give me what I need this day so that I can live as your child, not pleasing myself, but doing the good you have already prepared for me to do.

As my mind races through all I have to do in this one day, it is so easy to become pressured, to forget that you have planned my life and are always at hand to help me do your will.

Fill me with your gift of self-control throughout this day. Help me to grow in using those gifts of the Spirit which you have already provided like beautiful garments for me to wear.

Give to me also—
a good sense of humor;
cheerfulness in the face of difficulties;
the ability to be able to laugh at myself and not take myself too seriously;
and a sensitivity of spirit, to see quickly when I am hurting others and to avoid thoughtlessly trampling on their feelings.

This is a lot to ask for—but I do so confidently, through Jesus your Son, my Lord. Amen.

Thank you, God for today and all its enjoyments for me.

I know that in everything you work for good with those who love you, those whom you have called as your own, and so I know that all that happened today was for my good—even those things I did or said or thought which I didn't really mean and for which I ask your forgiveness.

I thank you—
for any lovely thing I have seen or enjoyed today;
for my loved ones without whom life would never be the same;
for those things that happened today which I really enjoyed and which made me feel that life is worth living;
for the laughter or tears that this day has brought to me;
for those events that helped me think more seriously about my life with you.

Watch over me as I now go to rest, and make me aware of your great love and forgiveness as I close my eyes in sleep.

In Jesus' name I pray. Amen.

Morning

Lord, when I wake up some mornings, I feel that it would be better not to have to go out to the day's work, while there are other mornings when I feel refreshed and ready to face a new day with enthusiasm. Whatever my feelings, I know that this is a new day and there are things that I have to do; so be with me, Lord, and help me to do well what I have to do.

Help me—
- to keep talking with you throughout today, especially when I am waiting with nothing special to do;
- to be appreciative of others so that I become known for praising people rather than criticizing them;
- to bite my tongue when it wants to run wild and say things that should never be said;
- to be quick to apologize before an argument, instead of waiting to the bitter end;
- to keep control when people say or do things that might irritate or unsettle me. May I always remember that to have gained my point is no prize when I have hurt a friend.

So help me, Lord, to grow more like you each day.

I pray for your love's sake. Amen.

Before I go to rest, I lift up my heart to praise you for all the goodness you show to me and those around me.

O God, I thank you—
    for my family;
    for my many friends;
    for the fellowship of your people I belong to;
    for the wonderful gift of your Holy Spirit who has
        filled me and poured out on me such glorious
        gifts, although I deserve nothing from you.

I am surely privileged to be a saint in your kingdom,
        covered by the merits of my dear Lord Jesus
        Christ, to be able to serve you and all the people
        that make up my life. It is good to be at home
        with you, dear God, through Jesus alone, and it
        is good to enjoy the discoveries of the many
        ways you show your will to me. Let me never
        cease to give praise, thanks, and glory to you for
        all these gifts.

Grant that other people may find that peace and joy
        in life that comes from you alone. Be in every
        home tonight to comfort, encourage, guide, and
        correct, and grant us all to feel your presence
        and know your love. Amen.

*G*ood morning, Lord!

Another day has dawned, and it is easy for me to feel tired and worn out even before I go to work. Help me to feel refreshed and encouraged to do what is required of me today, so that I can come to its end with satisfaction that under your direction I have done the best I could.

Lord, thank you that the power of the Holy Spirit comes to me through your Word—through the Bible and Holy Communion. I need lots of power in my life to cope with all that comes my way, and I ask you, Lord, to keep pouring that power into me, so that I not only scrape through each day but become excited as I discover your will for me and enjoy doing it as best I can.

Lord, forgive me for the mistakes I have made and the ones I'll make during this day.

Praise you, Lord, that the outpouring of your Holy Spirit is never cut off because we keep falling into the same dirty puddles again and again.

Thank you for my church—
    for its provisions for worship;
    for its pastor;
    for all the warmth of love that I enjoy so much.

Help me to walk this day, looking always to Jesus, whose I am, and whom I am continuing to serve. Amen.

Dear God, thank you for another day.

I know how much of its time flitted by, during
which I gave no thought of you. I am grateful
that you understand how it is with us on earth,
and you will never turn us away. For Jesus lived
here as one of us and he knew how it was to be
tempted. Help me to claim his victory and live a
victorious life over the old enemies of the devil,
the world, and my own sinful self.

Thank you now—
for happy things which came to me . . . unexpectedly;
for events which turned out better than I thought . . .
for difficulties which helped me to learn how to
face up to them and cope with them;
for all the wonderful people who bring joys to my
life.

Forgive me—
for the things I failed to do;
for forgetting to give encouragement to others by
words, by a letter, or by a telephone call;
for any promises which I have not yet kept;
for . . . decisions I keep putting off because I'm afraid;
for the bad habits . . . I have still not given up.

Help me to see myself as I really am, to be humble
enough to seek help, and, when I have received it,
to accept and apply it in the power of your grace.

For Jesus' sake, I pray. Amen.

O God, it is good to be alive and begin this day with you.

Help me to count my many blessings before I go out
to do what has to be done.

I thank you—
for life, and the health and strength to enjoy life;
for Jesus, his Word to me, his love for me, and his
power in me.
for the privilege of being born again and having
the assurance of abundant life now and forever;
for my home and those who are near and dear to me;
for the friends I will meet today, as I travel, at my
work, in the course of the day, and when the
day is done;
for all those things in which I find pleasure: my
work, recreation, hobbies, books, television,
music, dancing, talks with friends, and especially the fellowship I enjoy with those who are
dear to me.

Lord, there are so many things which could be added
to this short list, and for them all I thank you.

Watch over me this day so that I may return at its
end in safety and peace.

For Jesus' sake. Amen.

O Lord, it so often happens that I go out in the morning with good intentions to make the day a success, but it does not work out the way I had hoped and prayed.

I am sorry now for all my failures—
    for wasting time;
    for speaking harshly to others;
    for losing my temper with people;
    for blaming others when I should have taken the
      blame;
    for being disloyal to you, my Lord;
    for failing to pray, to meditate on your Word, and
      to spend more time in fellowship with you.

Thank you for extending your forgiveness to me. I love to hear you say to me each day: "Your sins are forgiven! Go in peace!"

Help me to sleep in peace, sure of your love and care which surrounds me; and grant that tomorrow I may wake up with a clear mind, a refreshed body, and a heart at peace with others and with you.

Through my Lord Jesus Christ. Amen.

PERSONAL PRAYERS

Copyright © 1984 by Openbook Publishers

Dimensions for Living edition published 2001

All rights reserved.

This book is printed on recycled, acid-free, elemental-chlorine– free paper.

Library of Congress Cataloging-in-Publication Data

Schreiber, Allan W.
   Personal prayers / Allan W. Schreiber.
      p. cm.
   ISBN 0-687-09918-8 (alk. paper)
   1. Prayers. I. Title.
 BV245 .S34 2001
 242'.8—dc21

2001032578

Scripture quotation noted TEV is from Today's English Version--Second Edition. Copyright © 1992 by American Bible Society. Used by permission.

01 02 03 04 05 06 07 08 09 10—10 9 8 7 6 5 4 3 2 1

MANUFACTURED IN THE UNITED STATES OF AMERICA